Playful Pet Projects

Get Crafting for Your
LOVELY
LIZARD

by Ruth Owen

BEARPORT
PUBLISHING

Minneapolis, Minnesota

CREATE!

Credits

Library of Congress Cataloging-in-Publication Data

Names: Owen, Ruth, 1967- author.
Title: Get crafting for your lovely lizard / by Ruth Owen.
Description: Minneapolis, Minnesota : Bearport Publishing Company, [2021] |
    Series: Playful pet projects | Includes bibliographical references and
    index.
Identifiers: LCCN 2020039229 (print) | LCCN 2020039230 (ebook) | ISBN
    9781647476649 (library binding) | ISBN 9781647476717 (ebook)
Subjects: LCSH: Lizards as pets—Equipment and supplies. | Pet
    supplies—Juvenile literature. | Handicraft—Juvenile literature.
Classification: LCC SF459.L5 O94 2021 (print) | LCC SF459.L5 (ebook) |
    DDC 745.5—dc23
LC record available at https://lccn.loc.gov/2020039229
LC ebook record available at https://lccn.loc.gov/2020039230

For more information, write to Bearport Publishing, 5357 Penn Avenue South, Minneapolis, MN 55419. Printed in the United States of America.

CONTENTS

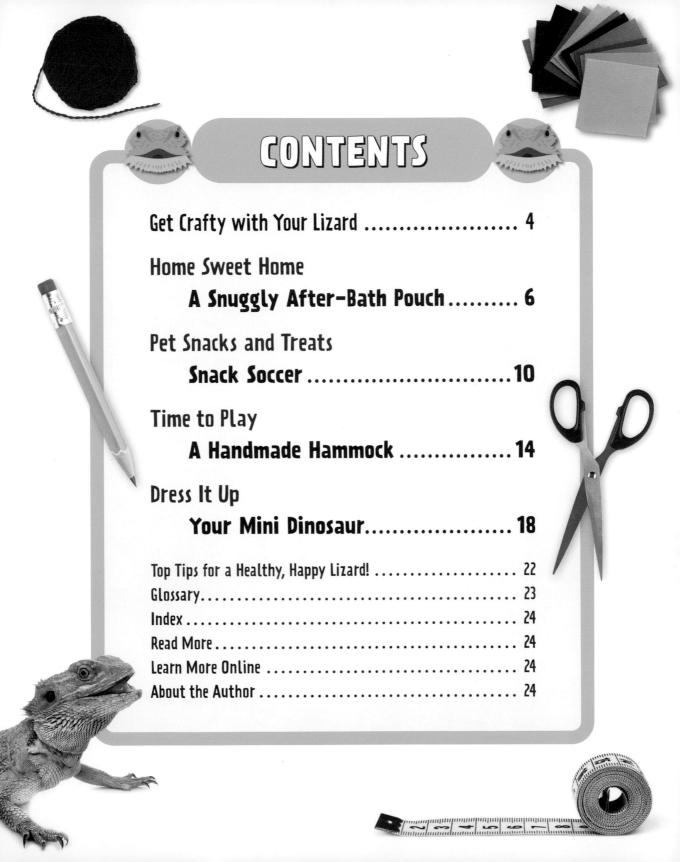

GET CRAFTY WITH YOUR LIZARD

If you share your home with a lizard and you enjoy crafting, this is the book for you! These crafts have been designed for bearded dragons, but if you're the proud parent of a different **species**, that's no problem. Every lovely lizard is welcome!

◀ Home Sweet Home

A lizard needs to stay clean to be healthy. This pouch will be perfect to keep your beardie cozy and warm after its regular bath.

Pet Snacks and Treats ▶

Lively lizards need to play to stay healthy. Make exercise exciting with one of these colorful paper balls with a delicious treat inside.

◀ Time to Play

A hammock is perfect for your lounging lizard! Learn how to **weave** one while you recycle some old T-shirts.

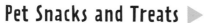

Dress It Up ▶

Lizards are **reptiles**. Many of the dinosaurs that lived on Earth were also reptiles. Turn your little lizard into one of its ancient **ancestors** with this delightful dinosaur costume!

Have Fun and Be Safe

Crafting for your lovely lizard can be lots of fun. But it's important that both you and your pet stay safe by following these top tips for careful crafting.

- Always get permission from an adult before making the projects in this book.

- Read the instructions carefully, and ask an adult for help if there's something you don't understand.

- Be careful when using scissors, and never let your lizard touch or play with them.

- Keep any glue where your pet can't sniff, lick, or touch it.

- When your project is complete, recycle any extra paper, cardboard, or packaging. Keep leftover materials for a future project.

- Clean up when you've finished working.

- Remember! Some bearded dragons do well being handled by their humans. But others seem to do best with only a little attention.

Never force your lizard to do something it seems unhappy to do.

A SNUGGLY AFTER-BATH POUCH

To stay happy and healthy, lizards need to be clean. Regular baths in warm, shallow water are important to keep your bearded dragon in tip-top shape. After a nice bath, this cozy pouch is the perfect place for your little dragon to stay snuggly warm while it dries off.

When giving your beardie a bath, think safety! Fill a sink or tub with enough water to reach only its shoulder, so your lizard can easily stand with its head out of the water.

You will need
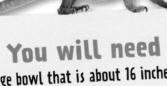

- A large bowl that is about 16 inches (40.6 cm) wide
- Thick fleece or an old towel
- A black marker
- Scissors
- A tape measure
- Sewing pins
- A needle
- Thread in a color that matches your fabric
- A thin foam pad that is at least 15 in (38 cm) wide
- A pencil or chalk to write with
- Colorful felt
- Tacky glue

6

1 Place the bowl on the back of your fabric and trace around it with the marker. Repeat two more times. Carefully cut out the three circles.

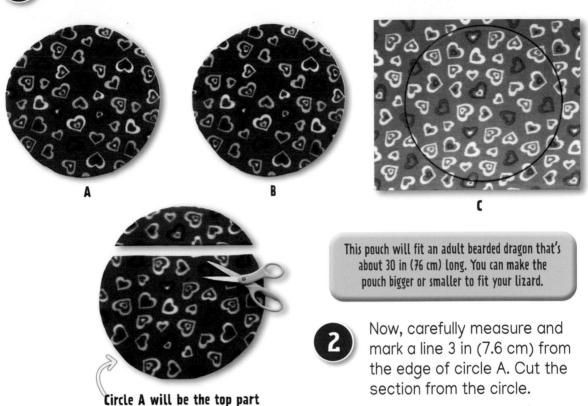

A

B

C

Circle A will be the top part of the pouch.

This pouch will fit an adult bearded dragon that's about 30 in (76 cm) long. You can make the pouch bigger or smaller to fit your lizard.

2 Now, carefully measure and mark a line 3 in (7.6 cm) from the edge of circle A. Cut the section from the circle.

3 Take circle A and fold over about ½ in (1.25 cm) of the cut edge to make a **hem**. The edge of the hem should be on the back of the fabric.

4 Pin the hem, and then carefully sew it with small, neat stitches. Remove the pins.

5 Now, lay circle B flat with the back of the fabric faceup. Place circle A on top of circle B, also with the back of the fabric showing. Pin the circles together along the overlapping circle edge.

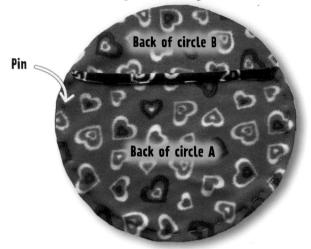

Pin

Back of circle B

Back of circle A

6 Carefully sew the edges of the two pieces together, stopping when you get to the hem. Remove the pins, and then turn the pouch right side out.

Front of circle B

Front of circle A

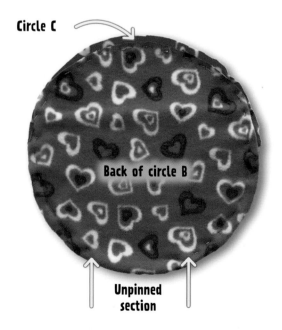

Circle C

Back of circle B

Unpinned section

7 Lay circle C flat with the front of the fabric faceup. Lay the piece you've just sewn from circles A and B on top of circle C with the back faceup. Pin the pieces together near the edges, leaving a space of about 4 in (10 cm) unpinned.

8 Carefully sew around the line of pins you've just made and then remove the pins. Turn the pouch right side out through the part that was not sewn.

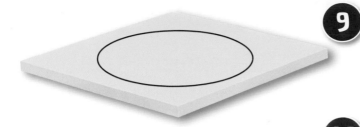

9 Next, lay the pouch on your piece of foam and trace around it with a pencil or chalk. Cut out the foam circle.

10 Squeeze the foam circle into the pouch through the section that was left open in steps 7 and 8.

Pinned section

11 Close up the unstitched section by tucking in the fabric as neatly as possible. Then, pin and sew this section closed. Remove the pins when you're done.

12 Finally, draw the letters of your lizard's name on felt. Carefully cut out the letters and glue them to the top of the pocket. The snuggle pouch is ready for after-bath lizard comfort.

BEAUTIFUL AFTER BATH!

SNACK SOCCER

In the wild, bearded dragons spend their days catching insects and **foraging** for plants to eat. A pet bearded dragon that spends most of its time in a tank needs things to do, too. Playing with toys, such as a treat-filled ball, is a good way to keep your beardie's body and brain active.

You will need
- 2 sheets of colored paper
- A ruler
- Scissors
- A non-toxic glue stick

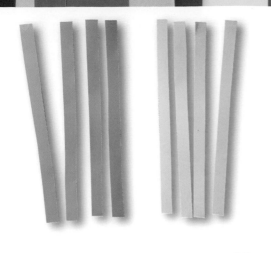

1. Begin by measuring and cutting eight strips of paper that are 8 in (20.3 cm) long and ½ in (1.25 cm) wide. Cut four strips in one color and four in the other color.

2. Next, fold the strips in half so the short ends meet. Crease, and unfold again.

3. Put a small dab of glue on the center fold of each strip.

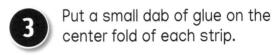

GLUE

4. Stick four strips of one color together in their centers to form a star shape.

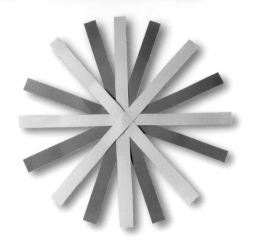

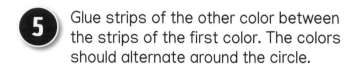
5 Glue strips of the other color between the strips of the first color. The colors should alternate around the circle.

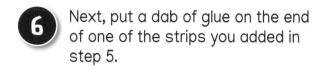
6 Next, put a dab of glue on the end of one of the strips you added in step 5.

7 Take both ends of the glued strip and join them together to form a loop. The ends should overlap by about ¼ in (0.6 cm). Then, add a dab of glue to the ends of all of the remaining strips.

8 Take another strip of the same color and stick the ends to the top of the loop you've just made, overlapping them by about ¼ in (0.6 cm). You will see that a ball shape is forming.

9 Continue forming circles with the rest of the strips of that color.

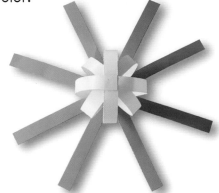

10 Next, add the strips of the other color to the top of the circle.

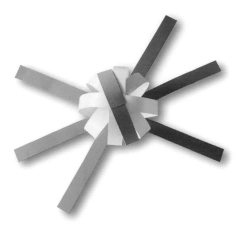

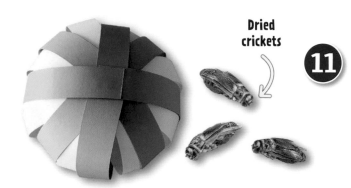

Dried crickets

11 When the paper ball is done, allow the glue to dry completely. Then, put a small piece of food, such as a dry cricket, inside the ball and offer it to your lizard.

WHO'S UP FOR SNACK SOCCER?

A HANDMADE HAMMOCK

Wild bearded dragons **clamber** over rocks and climb on tree branches to rest in the sun. Make sure your beardie's tank feels like its wild home with a hammock for resting. This will give your pet a nice place to spread out and **bask** under its heat lamp.

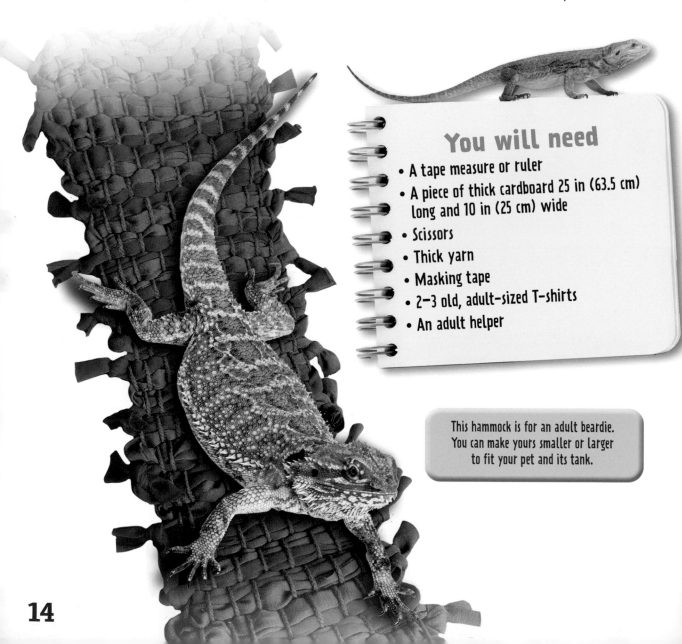

You will need

- A tape measure or ruler
- A piece of thick cardboard 25 in (63.5 cm) long and 10 in (25 cm) wide
- Scissors
- Thick yarn
- Masking tape
- 2–3 old, adult-sized T-shirts
- An adult helper

This hammock is for an adult beardie. You can make yours smaller or larger to fit your pet and its tank.

1 To make your weaving **loom**, cut 18 slots in each short end of the cardboard rectangle. Each slot should be ½ in (1.25 cm) deep and about ½ in (1.25 cm) apart. Make sure the slots at both ends line up with one another.

2 Slide the end of your yarn into the top right-hand slot on the loom. Then, tape the end of the yarn to the cardboard. This side will now be the back of the loom.

Slot

To make a larger hammock, the loom should be wider and have more slots.

Back of the loom

3 Turn the loom over. Wind the yarn down the front and into a bottom slot, then up the back and into the next top slot.

4 Keep winding until your yarn has made it through all the slots and the remainder is at the back of the cardboard.

Front of the finished loom

5 Give yourself a few extra inches and cut the yarn. Then, tape the end on the same side of the cardboard as your other taped end. Your loom is complete.

6 Cut your T-shirts into fabric strips that are about 1 in (2.5 cm) wide and the length of the body of the T-shirts.

7 Take a fabric strip. Starting in the top left-hand corner, weave it under the first strand of yarn, over the next strand, and under the third. Pull the strip through until there is about 3 in (7.6 cm) of fabric left hanging on the left-hand side. Then, keep weaving the strip over and under the yarn.

8 When you reach the end of the row, weave your strip back in the opposite direction. Weave the strip back under, and then continue to weave over and under.

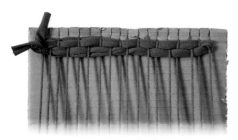

9 When you reach the end of the second row, push the fabric up toward the top of the loom so the two rows are tight together. Then, tie the two ends of the strip in a double knot and trim off any extra fabric.

10 Take a second strip and begin weaving it, this time starting from the right-hand side. Keep pushing the fabric rows tightly together.

11 Repeat steps 7 through 10 until the weaving fills the loom.

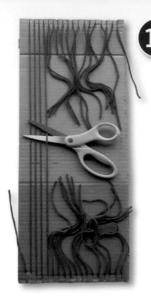

12 Turn the loom over. Undo the two ends of the yarn that were taped down, and cut through the center of the other strands of yarn.

13 Take the first two strands of yarn and tie them in a double knot. Keep tying the strands of yarn together in pairs. Trim off any extra yarn. Then, repeat on the other end of the hammock. Add strings to help hang your hammock, and it's all finished!

14 Ask an adult to help you find a place for the hammock in your lizard's home.

JUST HANGIN' OUT!

YOUR MINI DINOSAUR

Bearded dragons get their name from their dragon-like scales and their spiky throats that can puff out to look like a beard. Why not add some more spikes? Make an awesome outfit for your beardie, and dress it up as a fierce spiky dinosaur!

You will need
- An adult helper
- A tape measure
- A pencil
- Scrap paper
- Felt (in two different colors)
- Scissors
- 2 pairs of Velcro dots
- Tacky glue
- Tracing paper

Width

Length

1 Ask a helper to gently hold your lizard while you measure the length along its back from the neck to just in front of its back legs. Then, measure the width of its back at the widest part. Write down the measurements.

2 Next, very carefully and gently measure around your lizard's neck. Measure around its tummy, just in front of its back legs. Write down the measurements.

3 To make the fitted part of the costume, cut a rectangle of felt the size of your lizard's back measurements.

4 To make the costume's fastening strips, take some felt that's the same color as the fitted part. Cut a strip of felt that is ¼ in (0.6 cm) wide and the length of your lizard's neck measurement plus an extra ½ in (1.25 cm).

5 Then, cut a second ¼ in (0.6 cm) wide strip that is the length of the tummy measurement plus an extra ½ in (1.25 cm).

Neck strip

Tummy strip

6 Take a pair of Velcro dots. Stick one dot to each end of the neck strip, making sure that the strip forms a loop when the Velcro is stuck together. Repeat on the tummy strip.

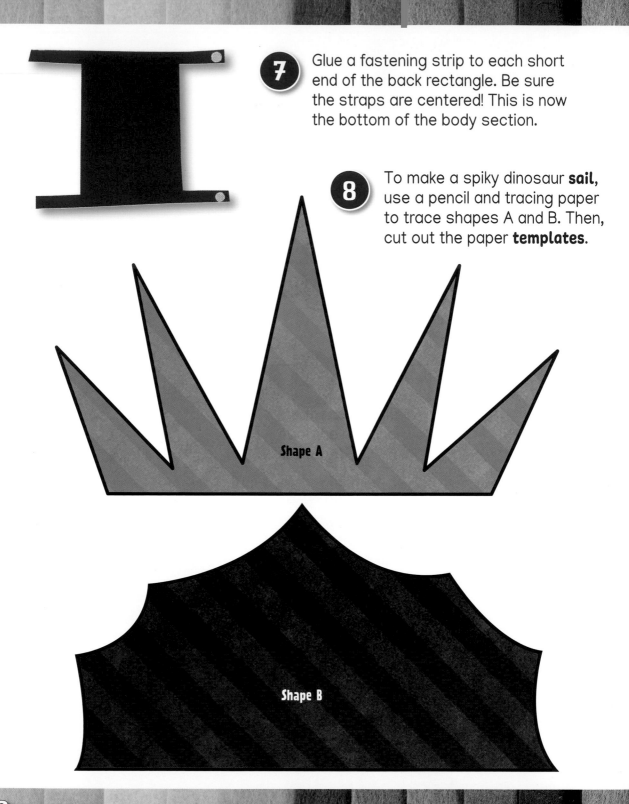

7 Glue a fastening strip to each short end of the back rectangle. Be sure the straps are centered! This is now the bottom of the body section.

8 To make a spiky dinosaur **sail**, use a pencil and tracing paper to trace shapes A and B. Then, cut out the paper **templates**.

Shape A

Shape B

Template

9 Lay template A on the same color felt as the body section. Trace around it with a pencil, and cut out the shape. Repeat to make a second felt shape A.

10 Now, lay template B on a different color of felt. Trace around the template in pencil, and cut out the shape.

11 Next, glue one felt shape A to each side of shape B. Make sure the points match up.

Shape A

12 Finally, put a line of tacky glue along the middle of the body section. Place the sail in the line of glue so it stands up straight. Allow the glue to dry.

13 When the glue is completely dry, it's time to turn your little lizard into a daring dinosaur.

RUN! IT'S A BEARDIE-O-SAURUS

Only dress up your beardie pal for a few minutes, and stop if it seems upset. Never leave your lovely lizard alone when it is wearing its dinosaur costume.

TOP TIPS FOR A HEALTHY, HAPPY LIZARD!

Being a **responsible** reptile owner is all about keeping your pet healthy. Here are 10 tips to help you take care of your lovely lizard.

1 Lizards are cold-blooded. This means they can't control their body temperature. In their tank, they need both a warm place and a cooler place so they can heat up or cool down.

2 At night, switch off all the lights in the room where your lizard lives so it can sleep.

3 Always be sure to give your lizard fresh, clean water each day.

4 Bearded dragons eat live insects and greens. Remove any leftover food from your pet's tank at the end of the day.

5 To prevent choking, be sure that any pieces of food you give your beardie are no larger than the space between its eyes.

6 Remove any poop from the tank as soon as your lizard goes to the bathroom.

7 In the wild, bearded dragons mostly live alone. It's best to have a single beardie living in a tank.

8 A bearded dragon sheds its skin as it grows. Never pull on shedding skin—you may damage the new skin underneath.

9 Gently pick up your lizard with both hands, and always support its four legs.

10 A bearded dragon may live for 10 to 15 years. Be sure you are willing to care for a lizard for all this time!

GLOSSARY

ancestors family members who lived a long time ago

bask to lie in warmth and light from the sun or a lamp

clamber to climb and move over objects slowly

foraging looking for food in the wild

hem the edge of a piece of fabric that has been turned over and sewn

loom a piece of equipment used for weaving fabric

reptiles cold-blooded animals, such as snakes and lizards, that have a backbone and scaly skin

responsible caring, trustworthy, and in charge

sail a large, flat body part that stands up on the back of an animal and looks a little like a boat's sail

species groups that animals are divided into because of similar characteristics

templates shapes that can be used for drawing and cutting around

weave to form by lacing together strands of material

INDEX

READ MORE

Andres, Marco. *Bearded Dragons (Our Weird Pets)*. New York: PowerKids Press, 2018.

Titmus, Dawn. *Reptiles and Amphibians (Cool Pets for Kids)*. New York: Rosen Publishing, 2019.

LEARN MORE ONLINE

1. Go to **www.factsurfer.com**

2. Enter "**Crafting Lizard**" into the search box.

3. Click on the cover of this book to see a list of websites.

ABOUT THE AUTHOR

Ruth Owen has been developing and writing children's books for more than 10 years. She lives in Cornwall, England, just minutes from the ocean. Ruth loves all animals—wild and pets. Her favorite fact about bearded dragons is that they can grow a whole new skin and then shed the old one!